W9-CUO-458

A MINDFUL APPROACH TO PARENTING

Insights on Raising Our Children With
Wisdom, Awareness, and Acceptance

Geoff Bell-Devaney

A Mindful Approach To Parenting
Insights on Raising Our Children With Wisdom, Awareness, and Acceptance

PUBLISHED BY **FREE DOG PRESS**

Printed in the United States of America
First Printing: October 2009
ISBN 144865971X

Inquiries to: freedogpress@yahoo.com

To Parker,

Words cannot express
how I feel...

AUTHOR'S NOTE

This is a book about parenting with acceptance, courage, and compassion. About being mindful of our own emotions and experiences, as well as those of our children. This is about acknowledging reality; the reality of life as it reveals itself to us in every moment, so that we can learn from it and grow in awareness, wisdom, and equanimity.

The life of a parent is not an easy one at times. But it is also the best one, at times. No matter how easy or difficult your journey may be, know that every moment is designed so that you can learn about yourself, and become a more compassionate, strong, and patient person.

Don't hide from the moments that your child provides you. Instead, embrace them in all their beauty and ugliness, and let them lead you unto yourself - allow them to help you better know yourself, so that you can grow in peace and understanding. So that you can do your best to be present for yourself and for your child.

Good luck!

Geoff Bell-Devaney

A Mindful Approach To Parenting
Insights on Raising Our Children With Wisdom, Awareness, And Acceptance

If your parenting style is based in patience and love it will never go out of fashion.

A child's emotions are always appropriate, even when their behaviors are not.

It is better to calm an angry child than to fight with him.

"Because I said so" is not a good enough reason.

Sometimes acting silly is the smartest thing to do.

Expecting your child to always do what you want is like expecting it to always be warm and sunny.

The only thing that yelling usually achieves is more frustration, hard feelings, and chaos.

You will have constant practice at being patient, until you become it.

When we look for our children
to be perfect, we fail to see how
they already are.

Never assume that a child
knows that what he is doing is
wrong.

Try to remember that your child is just a child.

Children are the essence and the expression of life - you can see it in their tears and hear it in their laughter.

Instead of yelling at your child, try telling her why you are angry.

Can you hear your child teaching you how to listen?

Being tired makes everything so much more difficult.

Let your child know that you love him, even when you don't like him.

Don't be afraid to let your child see you smile - it will teach him that it is okay to be happy.

Hitting a child only teaches her to live in fear.

Often, when it's all just beginning to make sense it changes.

Amongst the busyness, the joy of simplicity can be discovered.

Sometimes trying to make it all better only makes it worse.

A child can teach you to stay still when all you really want to do is run.

When your child is yelling, let her know it is okay to be angry.

A playful child can remind us that it's okay to have fun.

You might be amazed at how great it feels to simply be alone.

Just because the television is cheap and available, doesn't mean it's a good babysitter.

You may discover anger inside that scares you.

Being a parent can make you feel stronger than you ever have.

Being a parent can make you feel smaller than you ever have.

A child who is met with empathy learns to welcome all of their emotions.

When your child is scared,
let him know it is okay to be
afraid.

If you want your child to do
something, it helps to tell him
why.

If your child is acting out, she might just be needing an attentive audience.

Fighting with your child is a choice you are making.

You will never find a more rewarding career or a more inviting benefits package.

At times you will find yourself desperately looking forward to nap-time and bed-time.

It's okay to ask for help.

Setting healthy boundaries
can keep you from getting all
fenced in.

If you want children to respect your "no", you have to respect theirs.

A laughing child can remind us that it's okay to be happy.

Even if she is saying nothing, your child is listening.

Try to accept your child in every moment - for that is who she is.

Becoming a parent means a lot more than just having a child.

When your child is crying, let him know it is okay to be sad.

Anybody who thinks that raising a child is a piece of cake is out to lunch.

Too much love is never a bad thing.

Patience is the umbrella that keeps you dry during a child's emotional storms.

You will both envy and pity "stay at home" moms and dads.

Don't be afraid to show weakness to your child - it will teach him that it is okay to be vulnerable.

Never follow the advice of another parent until you first see how it feels to you.

Babies can be a real handful.

Letting your children be who they truly are is a great way of learning tolerance and understanding.

An angry child can remind us
that it's okay to be mad.

One way of staying open to life
is by accepting your child's ever
changing moods.

The newness and the sameness can be overwhelming.

It may seem, at times, as if life is mercilessly torturing you.

A Mindful Approach To Parenting

You'll know you're getting the hang of it when you don't mind getting up in the middle of the night.

You are now one of a multitude of dedicated, hardworking individuals who never receive a dime for their services.

If you thought your life was busy before you became a parent...

You don't become a good parent without making some bad mistakes.

Life chooses our children for
us, and we for them, so that we
can become whole.

Our own humanity is reflected
in our child's fears and desires.

Children are always making mistakes - just like their parents.

"Toughening up" a child doesn't make him stronger - it only makes him scared.

The terrible twos are also the
wonderful twos.

Because *you* are the adult,
you are the one who must try to
behave.

The constant interruptions
will leave you speechless.

Try listening to yourself
the next time you are yelling.

Your alarm clock will become more of a clock than an alarm.

A proud child can remind us that it's okay to acknowledge our accomplishments.

Children and adults aren't that much different - they both pretty much always think they're right.

The next time you feel like freaking out, try to remember that your child is learning from your example.

A power struggle can turn the smallest battle into the biggest war.

Imagine you were three feet tall and only knew a few hundred words.

One word can often be more effective than a long speech.

The next time your child says she has a problem, ask her how *she* might be able to fix it.

If a child always hears "no",
she may just stop asking.

Let go of wanting your child to
be like you, and let him be who
he is.

When you lose control,
remember that you can always
get it back.

Sometimes having to be a
parent can make you want to
act like a child.

Bath-time often involves a lot
of cleaning up.

Children aren't afraid to be
scared.

Avoid praising your child for every little thing lest she forgets to find encouragement within.

Teach your child that money does not equal love.

Don't be afraid to let your child
see your frustration - it will
teach her that life doesn't
always go our way.

If you thought adults' socks
got misplaced easily...

Don't let a broken vase do the same to your child's confidence.

A frightened child can remind us that it's okay to be scared.

When a child asks "why?", see if he knows the answer.

Simple toys make for creative children.

Lying to your child is a bit like stealing her money.

Time doesn't mean much to a child - except when it's time to go to bed.

Sometimes just getting out the door can be a journey unto itself.

Children don't pull their hair out over bad hair days.

You may find yourself fantasizing about adult-only retirement communities.

You aren't allowed to call in sick when your child is the boss.

Children have been known to design their whole day around the most unfashionable outfits.

You will need patience the most in those moments you are running out of it.

The main difference between being a good parent and a bad one is your degree of patience and level of attention.

A curious child can remind us to see life anew.

Your child's daily forecast calls for mostly sunny periods with occasional emotional out-pourings.

A child's procrastination often disguises itself as curiosity.

Kicking and screaming only makes it worse.

You will realize how much you don't know when your child starts looking to you for all the answers.

All of the crying can bring you to tears.

Trying to rush a child often only speeds up your frustration.

Because all children are unique, so are all parenting styles.

If you always give your child what she wants, she will become very good at taking.

Strong adults don't hit children, they protect them.

Don't be afraid to let your child see you care - it will teach him that it is okay to be compassionate.

Some days you would be willing to pay anything for some "free time".

Dreaming about the future often only makes the present worse.

We are all really just children trying to raise children.

Being a parent isn't quite so hard if you can stay soft inside.

A child needs to learn that kicking and screaming does not equal getting.

How do you like it when someone yells at you?

Trying to make a child sing in your key can ruin the whole song.

How can clothing that is so small be so expensive?

Most children are capable of violence, but can be taught to be peaceful.

If all children were taught to be peaceful, we could eliminate war within one generation.

Whoever said, "parenting is the hardest job" was absolutely right.

Children often cry over spilled milk.

Instead of pushing your child aside with advice, try making more room for their *own* discoveries.

Children may be small, but they can teach us that we are not bigger than life.

Try not to let your mean thoughts grow into mean actions.

Raising children can be both a dream and a nightmare.

Taking care of your own needs helps you better take care of others.

Yelling at your child is like cutting your own hair - it looks really bad and you walk around feeling stupid.

Wise parents aren't usually born that way.

Losing touch with your own playfulness can make parenting seem like a lot more work.

When you want to lash out try to remember that your child doesn't deserve your meanness.

Learning some effective parenting tools will make your whole life easier. And your child's.

A child's growing vocabulary shows how he is taking in everything we say.

To keep your child from stumbling is to keep her from growing.

At times you may be juggling so many things that you will start to feel like a street performer.

If you've been playing with the toys as well, they won't be so burdensome to clean up.

Become the mother or father you wish yours had been.

A crying child can remind us that it's okay to shed a tear.

Your child's constant "why's?"
can be really annoying - until
you realize that he truly doesn't
know.

No matter how much you may
want to, there is no way you
can protect your child from life.

Listening is often more important than talking.

Children can force us to think more about the future - and begin cherishing every moment.

Just because you are used to the violence on television, doesn't mean that your child is.

All of our ingenious ways of getting our child to eat more vegetables can get us eating more of them, too!

You may have to slow down just to keep up.

Children are the perfect antidote to boredom, selfishness, and laziness.

Children can be really immature.

Children can show us that things like matching socks aren't really as important as they seem.

It's easy to be a stern parent, but much more difficult to be open and vulnerable as well.

A child's laughter can melt away any seriousness.

Taking the time to be a good parent can mean there is a lot less of it left over for you.

When your child calls you by your first name, it can be very hard not to smile inside.

Your child can teach you the meaning of true love.

Don't be afraid to let your child see you crying - it will teach him that it is okay to be touched by life.

You might find yourself letting go of the unimportant things.

Eating in silence is a luxury enjoyed by monks, single people, and the deaf.

When you have a child it is a lot harder to just get up and go.

You may find yourself noticing flowers and other innocent things.

Be patient with yourself and your child - some things take a long time to figure out.

Playing with your child fairly can teach her to be a good sport.

It's easy to become over-
whelmed when we are resisting
the reality of our child's
emotions.

Trying to see your child as an
adult can help you embrace
their youth.

Although children are our most precious resource, the awareness of this seems to be a rather rare commodity.

You can often avoid a power struggle by empowering your child.

If you never agree to your child's plans you will miss out on some wonderful adventures.

A brave child can remind us to look beyond our fears.

Raising a child can teach you how to hold someone softly.

You will never truly be able to describe the joys and difficulties you are experiencing.

Your child will probably treat his spouse and children the same way that you treat yours.

Having a child provides one with a never ending supply of amusing stories to tell.

You will find it impossible to understand how anyone could hurt a child.

You will slowly begin to understand how someone could hurt a child.

Dressing a child can be like trying to get somewhere without a map – it's eventually going to happen, but it might just take a while.

You may find yourself looking at all children with a newfound wonder and respect.

There won't be much time to read a lot of big books, but there will be a lot of time to read the small ones.

You will sometimes want to call a "time-out" before the game has even begun.

Teach your child to comfort others by showing her comfort.

Children love to be the conductor of their own orchestra.

Taking a child to a fancy restaurant can be a recipe for disaster.

Experiencing a child's reality can be totally surreal.

Losing control can help you realize how balanced you are most of the time.

Discovering how smart children are can make you want to treat them like geniuses.

Stopping a child from playing is like stopping a bird from flying.

Finding your own way out of a difficult place can help you realize why children need their independence.

We can try so hard to get ahead in life that we leave our children behind.

Look within and you will discover a child.

Children are always ready to play - even when there's work to be done.

You may find yourself desperately wanting to believe that "it gets easier as they get older."

Try seeing things from your child's point of view.

It can sometimes be difficult to dance to the music that children want to play.

Teaching our children that a game is only a game can help us remember it, too.

Be careful not to alienate your child by crowding her space.

It is often best to let your child learn without too much interruption.

Teach your child to share by being generous with him.

If you can remember that you might not always know best, things will often work out a lot better.

We all wound our children in ways we do not see nor intend.

Each time you scream at your child, you push her a little bit further away.

Realizing that it is okay to say no to your child can be one of the hardest things.

Ignoring your child is a bit like leaving him alone in an empty room.

Shaming your child is a very small way to feel big.

We often yell at our children
so that we can feel strong.

It's better to melt into the
exhaustion than try to fight it.

Instead of trying to change your child, influence him through your actions.

You probably won't have much "spare time" to spare.

It is important to become familiar with your child's likes and dislikes - and respect them.

Watching a child open a present can make you feel like a kid again.

One reason we like children is because they are honest about their feelings.

Try speaking softly the next time you are angry.

The newness of it all can lead one toward humility and confidence.

Telling your child that you love him isn't enough - you have to show it.

If even one child lives in fear,
we have failed as a society.

Laughing and having a good
time are all well and fine,
but it is how you behave when
you are stressed out and angry
that perhaps counts the most.

Teaching your child to do the right thing is easiest when you are also doing it.

Even if you win the argument, you may lose your child's trust.

By learning to have compassion for our child, we can also learn to have it for ourselves.

Being present is the best present you can give your child.

Try to set aside some time for yourself each day.

Ask yourself what it truly means to be a parent.

When you are feeling overwhelmed, maybe let somebody know.

When you are yelling at your child, part of you may be screaming for help.

Before you know it, you will be all grown up.

A child's fears are real and must be acknowledged.

You can feel like screaming one minute and screaming for joy the next.

Remember that one day your child may be taking care of you.

There is a direct correlation between your level of happiness and your ability to accept your child in every moment.

The next time you are angry ask yourself if it's really all that important.

At times it can feel as if we are a slave to our child's tyranny.

Children don't care if you are tired when they want you to wake up.

If you can be a positive influence on your child, you will affect the whole world.

Try to shield your child from violence and hatred - they will discover it soon enough.

Children laugh at the funniest things.

Sometimes you can only stand back and let a tantrum run its course.

It is amazing how much a child can accomplish if given the opportunity.

Children need to be taught that they don't always come first.

Making space for yourself gives you more room inside.

If we could all cry like our children, we would live in a much happier world.

The first time your child uses
the word "kill", part of you may
die inside.

Remember to put down your
evening paper and listen to
your child's news.

Children are born with two great gifts - the ability to cry, and to be silent.

Sometimes your child will make you so angry that all you'll be able to do is laugh.

Children seem to be loudest
in those moments we want
them to be quietest.

Too much candy never made
any child sweeter.

Noticing how we often want our child to move faster can make us learn to slow down.

Once in a while, let your child plan the whole day.

Children love choices.

It is amazing how children can suddenly become full when they want to get up from the table.

Raising a child can teach you that life is about more than just having fun.

Children often resist being told what to do - and rightly so.

Children don't need money to be happy.

Trying to stay in shape can be an exercise in frustration.

Your child will introduce you to life if you let him.

Because it is hard to take from children, they can teach us to give.

Our children don't belong to us
- we just watch over them for a
little while.

Children don't try to
understand life - they just live
it.

You can't really tell a child to "grow up".

Teach your child the art of compromise and she will learn to respect herself and others.

Children can show us that it's okay to have an argument and still be best friends.

Children need to be challenged - and to challenge.

Children call it like they see it - even when it doesn't have a name.

When children ask if they can help, you often become the helper.

Confronting a child when she is misbehaving can teach her integrity and responsibility.

Considering how little they eat, it's amazing how much energy children have.

A timid child can remind us that it's okay to feel shy.

Listen to your child - she deserves to be heard.

Children grow up so fast
that you can hardly see it.

It's hard to be in the game
when you parent from the
sidelines.

When children run around a lot during the day, they sleep a lot better at night.

Try to hear what your child is saying behind his words.

A child sees things from the perspective of someone who knows little about fear or failure.

Try to earn your child's respect, instead of expecting it.

Watching your child grow can teach you how to embrace change.

Children are really good at bringing out the best and the worst in adults.

If you never let your child say "no", how will she be comfortable doing so when she really has to?

Working hard to be a good parent is a real labor of love.

Just because your child is on an emotional roller coaster doesn't mean that you have to get on it with him.

You will understand your parents' frustrations, and have even more respect for them.

It's easier to see eye to eye with your child if you get down on your knees when speaking to him.

It's perfectly okay to be unwilling to let your child do certain things.

Never dismiss your child's fears, lest they grow like unattended weeds.

If you don't teach your child to pick up after herself you can quickly begin to feel very scattered.

Sometimes having an hour or two to yourself can make everything seem better.

If you want your child to lead a fulfilling life, teach her to follow her own path.

Encourage your child to compete against himself.

When you are feeling defeated, remember that you are not helpless.

Put anything you want to hold on to well out of reach.

You might discover your mother or father in your own actions.

Become one with the moment and you will become one with life.

Children need to learn that we love them for who they are - not what they do.

A Mindful Approach To Parenting

Sometimes life can feel like a circus - with you as the ringmaster.

No thermometer can gauge the degree of compassion you feel when your child is sick.

If you always motivate your child with money, he can quickly become poor at doing anything without it.

Being creative is a great way to raise a child.

Letting your child have his own opinions can teach him to think for himself.

Because children are always changing, so must our approach to raising them.

You can always tell which
parents are busy and stressed
out - the ones with children.

See if your child can solve
any of your little problems.

Unconditional love doesn't mean letting your child hurt you.

Saying something louder often only makes it harder to hear.

Try to see the best in your child, even when she isn't showing it.

By giving your child the gift of self-awareness, you are giving him the keys to his future.

ABOUT THE AUTHOR

Geoff Bell-Devaney is a graduate of the Mindfulness Based Stress Reduction Teacher Training program at the University of Massachusetts Medical School. He is a public school Special Education teacher who has been practicing yoga and meditation for over ten years. He is the father of a wonderful son who was the inspiration for this book and the instructor of much of the wisdom in it.

12544870R00102

Made in the USA
Lexington, KY
13 December 2011